A TRUE BOOK™

ABOARD THE TITANIC

John H. Son

Children's Press®
An imprint of Scholastic Inc.

Content Consultant
Tim Maltin, *Titanic* author and historian

Library of Congress Cataloging-in-Publication Data
Names: Son, John, author.
Title: Aboard the Titanic/John H. Son.
Other titles: True book.
Description: First edition. | New York: Children's Press, an imprint of Scholastic, Inc., 2022. | Series: A true
    book | Includes bibliographical references and index. | Audience: Ages 8–10 | Audience: Grades 4–6 |
    Summary: "Next set in A TRUE BOOK series. Young readers rediscover the story of the largest and most
    luxurious ship ever built, The Titanic. Featuring historical imagery, first-hand accounts, and lively text"—
    Provided by publisher.
Identifiers: LCCN 2022002249 (print) | LCCN 2022002250 (ebook) | ISBN 9781338840506 (library binding)
    | ISBN 9781338840513 (paperback) | ISBN 9781338840520 (ebk)
Subjects: LCSH: Titanic (Steamship)—Juvenile literature. | Titanic (Steamship)—Employees—Juvenile
    literature. | Ocean travel—Juvenile literature. | Ocean liner passengers—North Atlantic Ocean—Juvenile
    literature. | Shipwrecks—North Atlantic Ocean—Juvenile literature. | Shipwreck victims—Juvenile
    literature.
Classification: LCC G530.T6 S644 2022 (print) | LCC G530.T6 (ebook) | DDC 910.9163/4—dc23/
    eng/20220221
LC record available at https://lccn.loc.gov/2022002249
LC ebook record available at https://lccn.loc.gov/2022002250

10 9 8 7 6 5 4 3 2 1   23 24 25 26 27

Printed in China 62
First edition, 2023

Design by Kathleen Petelinsek
Series produced by Spooky Cheetah Press

**Front cover: The mighty *Titanic*; passengers Masabumi
Hosono (top) and the Laroche family (bottom)**

Back cover: Fifth Officer Harold Lowe's whistle

Find the Truth!

Everything you are about to read is true *except* for one of the sentences on this page.

Which one is **TRUE**?

T or F   The *Titanic*'s youngest surviving passenger was nine years old.

T or F   The band continued to play as the *Titanic* sank.

Find the answers in this book.

What's in This Book?

Most of the *Titanic*'s female crew members took care of female passengers.

In addition to wooden lifeboats like these, the *Titanic* carried four collapsible lifeboats made of canvas.

The **BIG** Truth

Survival by the Numbers

Which passengers had the best chance of survival? 26

4 All Hands on Deck

What jobs did crew members have on board the *Titanic*? 29

Passenger Fang Lang survived by clinging to a piece of wood floating in the icy ocean.

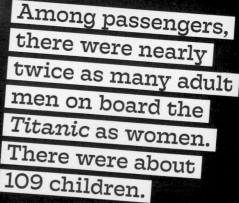

All Aboard!

Most people have heard of the **ship called the Titanic** and the **tragic tale of its sinking** on the night of **April 14–15, 1912**, after hitting an iceberg. The story is famous around the world. But history is filled with shipwrecks, including some that had a much greater loss of life. So why are people still fascinated by the *Titanic*, more than **100 years after it sank?**

Among passengers, there were nearly twice as many adult men on board the *Titanic* as women. There were about 109 children.

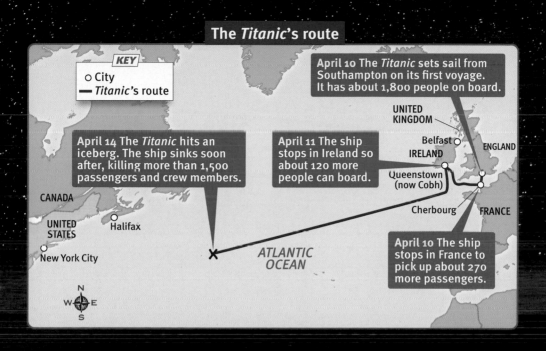

The *Titanic*'s route

KEY
○ City
— *Titanic*'s route

April 10 The *Titanic* sets sail from Southampton on its first voyage. It has about 1,800 people on board.

April 14 The *Titanic* hits an iceberg. The ship sinks soon after, killing more than 1,500 passengers and crew members.

April 11 The ship stops in Ireland so about 120 more people can board.

April 10 The ship stops in France to pick up about 270 more passengers.

UNITED KINGDOM

Belfast ○
IRELAND
Queenstown (now Cobh)
ENGLAND
Cherbourg
FRANCE

CANADA
UNITED STATES
Halifax ○
New York City ○
ATLANTIC OCEAN

N W E S

The *Titanic* was **world-famous** long before it set sail. After all, the *Titanic* and its twin ship, the *Olympic*, were the **largest ships ever built** at that time. And the most **luxurious**.

Many people **believed the *Titanic* could not sink**. But it did—on its very first voyage. Ever since that fateful night, the *Titanic*'s story has continued to grow in people's imagination. This is the story of the **passengers and crew members** who were aboard the *Titanic* on that tragic night.

The most expensive first-class ticket cost up to $4,350 (about $125,000 today). That is more than what a crew member would earn in 18 years!

R.M.S. "TITANIC"
APRIL 14, 1912

FIRST CLASS DINNER

HORS D'OEUVRE VARIES
OYSTERS
CONSOMME OLGA   CREAM OF BARLEY
SALMON, MOUSSELINE SAUCE, CUCUMBER
FILET MIGNONS LILI
SAUTE OF CHICKEN LYONNAISE
VEGETABLE MARROW FARCIE
LAMB, MINT SAUCE
ROAST DUCKLING, APPLE SAUCE
SIRLOIN OF BEEF   CHATEAU POTATOES
GREEN PEAS   CREAMED CARROTS
BOILED RICE
PARMENTIER & BOILED NEW POTATOES
PUNCH ROMAINE
ROAST SQUAB & CRESS
RED BURGUNDY
COLD ASPARAGUS   VINAIGRETTE
PATE DE FOIE GRAS
CELERY
WALDORF PUDDING
PEACHES IN CHARTREUSE JELLY
CHOCOLATE & VANILLA ECLAIRS
FRENCH ICE CREAM

A first-class dinner menu

This was the first-class smoking room.

First-Class Passengers

Experts estimate that when the *Titanic* left Europe for New York, there were 1,317 passengers on board. They were divided into three classes: first, second, and third. The 324 first-class passengers were rich. Some were also famous. They included millionaires, authors, entertainers, athletes, and fashion designers. First-class passengers enjoyed special features on the *Titanic*, including a swimming pool, a library, and even a spa.

Many of the first-class female passengers left the *Titanic* still wearing the evening clothes they had worn to dinner.

Titanic's Richest Passenger

American John Jacob Astor was the richest person traveling on the *Titanic*. In fact, at the time, he was among the richest people in the world. Astor was best known for building large, luxurious buildings like the Astor Hotel in New York City. He was sailing with his pregnant wife, Madeleine, their three servants, and their beloved dog, Kitty. When the ship began to sink, Astor helped his wife and the servants crawl through a window onto one of the last lifeboats to leave the ship. He never made it off the *Titanic*.

They Would Not Be Parted

Isidor and Ida Strauss were an American couple returning from a long vacation in France. They had been married for 41 years and had seven children together. Isidor was best known for being a co-owner of the Macy's department store in New York City. Ida became famous for refusing to separate from her husband when it was time for her to board a lifeboat. Ida gave her fur coat to her maid and insisted she get on the lifeboat instead. Isidor and Ida were last seen holding each other close as the *Titanic* slipped beneath the waves.

There is an Isidor and Ida Strauss memorial plaque inside the Macy's department store in New York City.

11

Titanic's Chief Designer

As the ship's chief designer, Thomas Andrews knew every detail about the *Titanic*. He was on board for the first voyage to make sure everything was working well. Passengers often saw Andrews strolling along, writing in the notebook that he always carried. He was writing ideas for improvements to the ship. Shortly after the *Titanic* struck the iceberg, Andrews reached a stunning conclusion. The ship would sink in less than two hours. He spent that time urging as many passengers as he could find to put on their life vests and get into lifeboats. Andrews did not make it off the ship.

When the *Titanic* was being designed, Thomas Andrews recommended that the ship carry at least 48 lifeboats. It ended up with just 20—not nearly enough to save everyone on board.

Missing the Boat

A surprising number of people who had tickets for the *Titanic*'s first voyage missed the trip. Milton S. Hershey of the Hershey Chocolate Company had to reschedule his family's trip because he was busy at work. Several other people decided not to travel on the *Titanic* after apparently having bad dreams about the trip. And the entire London Symphony Orchestra was supposed to have been on the *Titanic*. Thanks to a change in their performing schedule, they traveled a week earlier.

Milton S. Hershey

Eva Hart and her parents were traveling in second class on the *Titanic*. She and her mother survived.

WHITE STAR LINE

TRIPLE SCREW STEAMER "TITANIC."

2ND. CLASS

APRIL 14, 1912.

DINNER.

CONSOMMÉ TAPIOCA

BAKED HADDOCK, SHARP SAUCE

CURRIED CHICKEN & RICE
SPRING LAMB, MINT SAUCE
ROAST TURKEY, CRANBERRY SAUCE

GREEN PEAS   PURÉE TURNIPS

BOILED RICE

BOILED & ROAST POTATOES

PLUM PUDDING

WINE JELLY   COCOANUT SANDWICH

AMERICAN ICE CREAM

NUTS ASSORTED

FRESH FRUIT

CHEESE   BISCUITS

COFFEE

A second-class dinner menu

Passengers in second class paid about $65 (about $1,900 today) for their tickets.

Second-Class Passengers

Second-class cabins on the *Titanic* were not as luxurious as first-class cabins. But they were comfortable and elegant. In fact, they were more luxurious than first-class accommodations on most other **ocean liners** of the time. The 284 passengers in second class included tourists, teachers and professors, members of the **clergy**, and **middle-class** families. They spent their time socializing or reading in the library and playing deck games like ring toss.

The *Titanic* was the first ship of its kind to have an electric elevator for second-class passengers.

The Laroche family

Far From Home

Joseph Philippe Lemercier Laroche and his two daughters were the only Black passengers on the *Titanic*. Laroche, who was born in Haiti, went to France at the age of 15 to earn a degree in engineering. He married a white woman named Juliette Lafargue and settled in France.

The Laroche family faced discrimination in France, however, and decided to move to Haiti. Their trip on the *Titanic* was the first part of that journey. Laroche's daughters were Simonne, who was three at the time of the trip, and Louise, who was one. After the ship hit the iceberg, Laroche helped his wife and daughters onto a lifeboat. He disappeared with the *Titanic*.

Staying Behind

Father Thomas Byles was an English priest. He was traveling on the *Titanic* to attend his brother's wedding in New York. On the morning of Sunday, April 14, Father Byles held Catholic services for passengers in second class, and then later in third class. That evening, he happened to be walking on the upper deck when the *Titanic* struck the iceberg. Byles spent the last hours of his life guiding passengers up from the third-class deck to the top deck, where they could make it to the lifeboats. Survivors remembered him calmly offering words of comfort and encouragement throughout the panic and confusion.

According to witnesses, Father Byles was offered a seat on a lifeboat. He chose to stay and give comfort to the people who weren't able to make it onto lifeboats instead.

Masabumi Hosono

Masabumi Hosono was the
lone Japanese passenger on
the *Titanic*. Masabumi was
asleep when the ship struck
the iceberg. His first
attempts to reach the
lifeboats were blocked by a
crew member who thought
Masabumi was a third-class
passenger. Eventually, Masabumi

Like a number of men who survived the sinking, Masabumi Hosono was later seen by some as a coward for saving his own life.

was able to make his way up to the
boat deck. As he watched women and children
being helped onto lifeboats, Masabumi heard an
officer shout, "Room for two more!" A man
immediately leaped onto a lifeboat and Masabumi
jumped in after him. He survived.

Women and Children First

In 1852, 60 years before the *Titanic* sank, a ship called the HMS *Birkenhead* was wrecked off the coast of South Africa. The captain ordered that the 26 women and children on board be saved first. Hundreds of soldiers left on the ship did not survive. The actions of the men were popularized in stories, and "women and children first" became a **maritime** tradition in cases of disaster. It is important to note that it is a tradition but not a law. When the *Titanic* began to sink, Captain Edward John Smith instructed crew members to place women and children in the lifeboats *first*. Some crew members thought that *only* women and children were allowed onto the lifeboats. Hundreds of seats were left empty as the lifeboats were lowered into the freezing waters.

About 700 people made it onto the ship's 20 lifeboats. There was room for at least 400 more.

WHITE STAR LINE

R.M.S. "TITANIC"   APRIL 14, 1912

THIRD CLASS

BREAKFAST

OATMEAL PORRIDGE & MILK
SMOKED HERRINGS, JACKET POTATOES
HAM & EGGS
FRESH BREAD & BUTTER
MARMALADE   SWEDISH BREAD
TEA   COFFEE

DINNER

RICE SOUP
FRESH BREAD   CABIN BISCUITS
ROAST BEEF, BROWN GRAVY
SWEET CORN   BOILED POTATOES
PLUM PUDDING, SWEET SAUCE
FRUIT

TEA

COLD MEAT
CHEESE   PICKLES
FRESH BREAD & BUTTER
STEWED FIGS & RICE
TEA

SUPPER

GRUEL   CABIN BISCUITS   CHEESE

Any complaint respecting the Food supplied, want of attention or incivility,
should be at once reported to the Purser or Chief Steward. For purposes of
identification, each Steward wears a numbered badge on the arm.

Third-class passengers were served full meals. On some other ships, steerage passengers had to bring their own food!

Third-class passengers paid about $36 (around $1,000 today) for a ticket.

20

Third-Class Passengers

More than half the passengers on board the *Titanic* traveled in third class, which was also called **steerage**. Most of the 709 third-class passengers were **emigrants** hoping to start new lives in the United States and Canada.

In many cases, emigrants traveled with their entire families. Cabins slept two to six people in bunk beds, so families could often stay together. Some passengers brought musical instruments, which they would play for their fellow travelers.

A Close Call

Nine-year-old Willie Loch Coutts was traveling with his mother and younger brother from London, England. They were looking forward to joining Willie's father, who had already moved to Brooklyn, New York. But Willie almost didn't make it there. He happened to be wearing a straw hat when the ship hit the iceberg. The hat made Willie look like an adult. At first, the ship's officers wouldn't let Willie join his mother and brother on a lifeboat. Thankfully, his mother was able to convince a crew member that Willie was young enough to get into the lifeboat, too.

Animals Aboard the *Titanic*

Humans weren't the only passengers aboard the *Titanic*. There was also a variety of animals taking the trip. The *Titanic*'s official mascot was a cat named Jenny. She lived in the **galley**, or the ship's kitchen. Twelve dogs traveled with first-class passengers on the *Titanic*. If the owners were busy, stewards were assigned to walk the dogs. Three of the dogs survived because they were small enough to be smuggled onto lifeboats by their owners. There were even four chickens on board! They were stored in the ship's **cargo hold** and did not survive the sinking.

A dog show had been planned for the day after the sinking.

Facing Discrimination

Fang Lang was one of eight Chinese men traveling in steerage. After landing in New York, they'd planned to continue on to Cuba. Five of the men made it onto a lifeboat. Fang Lang jumped into the freezing ocean and was able to climb onto a piece of floating wood. He was picked up by a lifeboat.

The Chinese passengers were Ah Lam, Fang Lang (pictured), Len Lam, Cheong Foo, Chang Chip, Ling Hee, Lee Bing, and Lee Ling. Len Lam and Lee Ling did not survive the wreck.

When the survivors made it to New York, the Chinese men were not allowed to come ashore to receive medical attention. The Chinese Exclusion Act of 1882 had made it illegal for Chinese immigrants to enter the United States. They had to stay on the rescue ship until their ship to Cuba was ready to leave.

Titanic's Youngest Survivor

Unlike other survivors of the *Titanic*, Millvina Dean didn't have any memories of being on the ship. That is because she was only nine weeks old at the time. In fact, Dean was the youngest passenger to survive the accident. She was emigrating to Kansas along with her parents and older brother. Dean's father did not make it off the *Titanic*, however. Later, Dean's mother brought her and her brother back to England. Dean didn't learn about her place in history until she was eight years old.

Like Millvina Dean, most of the children traveling on the *Titanic* were third-class passengers.

Survival by the Numbers

The list of passengers who survived the sinking of the *Titanic* tells a clear story. The ship's first-class passengers were in the best position to be saved. The rates of survival dropped from there. Passengers' locations on the ship are just part of the story of why that happened.

Cross Section of the *Titanic*

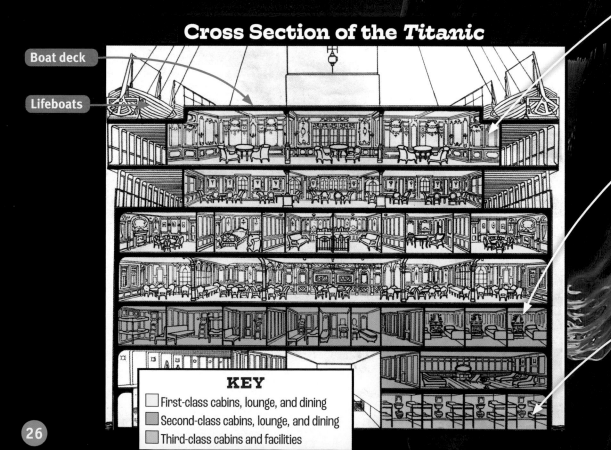

Boat deck

Lifeboats

KEY
- ☐ First-class cabins, lounge, and dining
- ☐ Second-class cabins, lounge, and dining
- ☐ Third-class cabins and facilities

First-Class Passengers

SURVIVAL RATE: 62%

Many first-class cabins were located on the highest part of the ship, so they were closest to the boat deck. That is where the lifeboats were. Of the 324 passengers in first class, 202 survived.

Second-Class Passengers

SURVIVAL RATE: 42%

The second-class cabins were not as close to the lifeboats as the cabins for first class were. Of the 284 second-class passengers on board, only 118 survived.

Third-Class Passengers

SURVIVAL RATE: 25%

The third-class cabins were located very far from where the lifeboats were being launched. But that is just part of the story. Many third-class passengers were traveling in large family groups of all ages and genders, and with all their belongings on the ship. Women were reluctant to leave their husbands, older children, and possessions on the ship. Many chose to remain together rather than head for the lifeboats alone. Of the 709 passengers in steerage, only 178 people survived.

All the female crew members survived the wreck.

All Hands on Deck

The crew members of the *Titanic* were responsible for operating the ship and taking care of its passengers. There were 908 crew members, 23 of whom were female stewards.

Many crew members sacrificed their lives to save passengers. Sadly, many of their individual stories were also lost. In the end, only 215 crew members survived the disaster.

More than 720 of the ship's crew were from Southampton, England, where the voyage began.

Going Down with His Ship

Captain Edward John Smith had the biggest job on board the *Titanic*. He was responsible for every part of the voyage and the ship. Smith set the ship's course and speed, directed all the crew members, and made sure proper procedures were followed. He was also ultimately responsible for the safety of his passengers. The captain is the person in charge, and so is always the last to leave a ship in a disaster. Captain Smith went down with the ship.

The *Titanic* had eight officers on board. Four of them survived.

Smith, who had been a professional sailor for 40 years, was close to retirement at the time of the *Titanic*'s voyage.

Crow's nest

Frederick Fleet was one of six lookouts on the *Titanic*. The men worked in pairs during two-hour shifts.

On the Lookout for Danger

A lookout's job is to keep a sharp eye on the waters in front of the ship all day and all night. On the night of the crash, Frederick Fleet and his partner, Reginald Robinson Lee, climbed the ladder to the **crow's nest**. Nearly two hours later, Fleet saw an iceberg appear out of the dark. He rang the crow's nest bell three times and called in a warning to the **bridge**. After the crash, Fleet helped passengers into lifeboats. He was then ordered to help row one of the boats, which allowed him to survive the sinking.

Getting the Message Out

Wireless operators Jack Phillips and Harold Bride worked and slept in the radio room—which was called the Marconi room. Once the ship began to sink, the men worked tirelessly sending messages for help and providing the ship's location. The distress call made it to a nearby ship, the *Carpathia*, which was able to sail to the rescue. Just before the *Titanic* sank, both operators plunged into the icy waters. Bride survived, but Phillips did not.

Timeline: The Crew on the Night of the Disaster

11:40 p.m.
Lookout Frederick Fleet spots the iceberg.

12:00 a.m.
Chief designer Thomas Andrews tells Captain Smith the ship will sink in about two hours.

12:05 a.m.
Captain Smith gives the order to prepare the lifeboats.

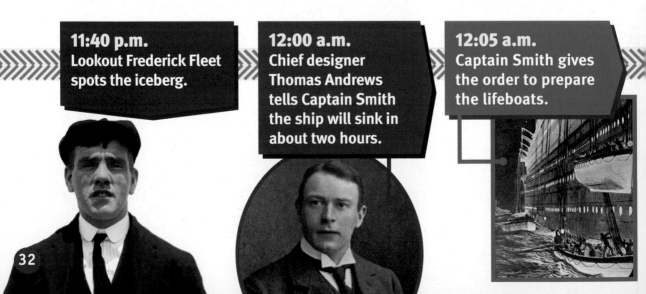

The Band Played On

The eight members of the *Titanic* orchestra were not part of the ship's "regular" crew. They were hired to perform during this voyage. Bandmaster and violinist Wallace Hartley led a quintet (five musicians) that played at evening meals and religious services. The other three musicians formed a trio that played in the first-class reception room. Famously, all eight musicians played throughout the sinking of the ship to calm and encourage the passengers and crew. None of the musicians survived.

12:20 a.m.
The *Carpathia*, a nearby ship, receives the distress calls from the wireless operators.

2:03 a.m.
The *Titanic*'s band moves from the first-class lounge to the deck and continues to play.

2:20 a.m.
Chief Baker Charles Joughin is the last person to leave the ship.

4:30 a.m.
The *Carpathia* arrives at the scene of the accident to collect survivors.

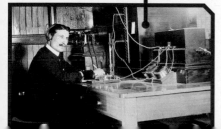

There were 24 double-ended coal-burning boilers on the *Titanic*. It could get as hot as 120 degrees Fahrenheit (49 degrees Celsius) inside the ship's large boiler rooms.

This photo shows **stokers** loading coal into a ship's boilers.

Keeping the Lights On

Engineers were responsible for keeping the engines and other equipment working. When the ship began taking on water, Chief Engineer Joseph Bell and his crew stayed belowdecks to help keep the ship's lights and wireless radio working for as long as possible. By the time the engineers came up to the boat deck, all the lifeboats were gone. They did not survive the shipwreck.

The Brave Baker

Chief Baker Charles Joughin was in charge of 13 bakers. He was resting in his bunk when he felt the collision. Once Joughin heard that the crew was preparing to launch the lifeboats, he ordered his bakers to provide bread from the storerooms for each boat. After helping place passengers onto the lifeboats, Charles tossed dozens of deck chairs overboard to be used as flotation devices. Just before the *Titanic* disappeared, Charles was able to step off the ship and swim in the icy waters for more than two hours before he was rescued.

Deck chair

Charles Joughin's survival was remarkable. Most people who ended up in the freezing water died quickly.

Miss Unsinkable

As a stewardess in first class, Violet Constance Jessup spent her days on the *Titanic* cleaning cabins, making beds, and serving tea. On the night of the crash, Jessup was reading in bed when she heard a "crunching, ripping sound." When she went up to the boat deck, Jessup was told to help passengers put on life vests and board the lifeboats. After surviving the sinking of the *Titanic*, Jessup worked on its sister ship the *Britannic*, which then sank during World War I. Incredibly, she survived that wreck as well.

Violet Constance Jessup's fame for surviving the sinking of two ships earned her the nickname "Miss Unsinkable."

Lost Mail

In addition to being the world's greatest luxury ocean liner of its time, the *Titanic* was also a floating post office. Its official name was the RMS *Titanic*—*RMS* stands for "Royal Mail Ship." Five postal clerks worked on the ship. Their job was to sort the mail from the more than 3,000 mailbags that were brought on board the ship, as well as mail posted by passengers and crew members during the trip. As the ship sank, the clerks tried to save all the mail sacks by moving them to the boat deck. Despite their efforts, all the mail went down with the ship. None of the clerks survived.

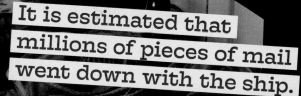

It is estimated that millions of pieces of mail went down with the ship.

A Life on the Sea

Harold Lowe began his life as a sailor when he was just 14 years old. Fifteen years later, he was hired as the fifth officer on the *Titanic*. The trip would be his first **transatlantic** voyage. While the ship was sinking, Lowe helped load passengers onto lifeboats before he was commanded to board one, too. After the *Titanic* completely disappeared beneath the waves, Lowe organized a team of rescuers to search for more survivors. Lowe and his crew pulled four people from the freezing water, three of whom survived.

Harold Lowe

Cries for help rang out in the pitch-black night. But without the lights of the *Titanic* to guide them, rescuers were unable to find many people.

A Ship of Stories

The story of the *Titanic* is not just one story about a shipwreck. The story of the *Titanic* is made up of more than 2,200 stories about the people who sailed on that doomed voyage. Many parts of the narrative came to light right away, including who survived and who perished. Some lay buried for many years. For

A *Titanic* lifeboat alongside the rescue ship, *Carpathia*

example, the fact that there were Black and Chinese passengers on board was largely forgotten or ignored. More than 100 years after this famous event, new research continues to add to the rich collection of stories about the *Titanic*.

Discovered Objects

We learn about the past through primary sources. These include objects or written materials that were created at the time of the event being studied. The wreck of the *Titanic* was discovered in 1985. Since then, many objects have been brought to the surface. They give us evidence of the experience of passengers and crew aboard the ship. Check out some of these fascinating objects!

Teacups

The first-class dishes and cups (left) were fancy. Those used in third class (right) were plainer and said "White Star Line," so they could be used on any of the company's ships.

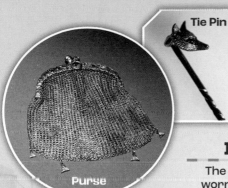

Tie Pin

Purse

Purse and Tie Pin

These fancy objects would have both belonged to first-class passengers.

Binoculars

These binoculars would have been used by lookouts.

Passengers' Hats

The top hat (left) would have been worn by a passenger in first class. Bowler hats (right) were used by working men at the time. This one likely belonged to a second-class passenger.

Bowler Hat

Top Hat

Whistle

Fifth Officer Harold Lowe's whistle made it off the ship with him.

Baker's Hat

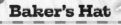

This baker's hat belonged to third baker William E. Hine.

LIFE ON THE *Titanic*

Marconi Room

The radio room is where the telegraph operators worked sending messages. It was named after Guglielmo Marconi, who invented the wireless telegraph system used on the ship.

Crow's Nest

The lookouts were stationed in the crow's nest 50 feet (15 meters) above the boat deck.

The Bridge

Gymnas
Read

First-Class Staircase

First-C

Squash Court

Post Office

Swimming Pool

Turkish Baths

First-Class Swimming Pool

Post Office

The *Titanic*'s mail clerks sorted as many as 60,000 pieces of mail a day!

First-Class Suite

Some first-class passengers enjoyed suites with private sitting rooms that were located through a set of doors from the bedroom.

Second-Class Cabin

Second-class passengers stayed in cabins that were comparable to first-class cabins on other ships.

Third-Class Cabin

Third-class passengers were crowded together in small—but nice—rooms.

Wilting Room | Reading Lounge | First Class Smoking Room | Verandah Café
First-Class Staircase | Á la Carte Restaurant | Second-Class Smoking Room
Library
Second-Class Dining
ception | First-Class Dining | Kitchen/Galley
Third-Class Dining | Third-Class Kitchen

Third-Class Dining

KEY
First-class cabins and facilities
Second-class cabins and facilities
Third-class cabins and facilities

True Statistics

Estimated number of passengers: 1,317

Number of first-class passengers: 324

Number of second-class passengers: 284

Number of third-class passengers: 709

Number of crew members: 908

Number of lifeboats: 20

Number of lifeboats successfully launched: 18

Total capacity of lifeboats: 1,178 people

Total number of survivors: 713

Did you find the truth?

F The *Titanic*'s youngest surviving passenger was nine years old.

T The band continued to play as the *Titanic* sank.

Resources

Other books In thls serles:

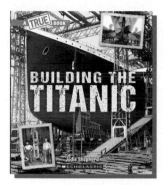
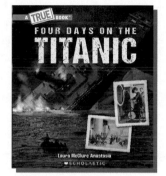
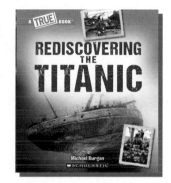

You can also look at:

Benoit, Peter. *The Titanic Disaster*. New York: Scholastic, 2011.

Montero, Mary. *Voices of the Titanic: A Titanic Book for Kids*. Emeryville, CA: Rockridge Press, 2019.

Ohlin, Nancy. *The Titanic*. New York: Little Bee Books, 2016.

Tarshis, Lauren. *I Survived the Sinking of the Titanic, 1912*. New York: Scholastic, 2010.

Zullo, Allan. *Titanic Young Survivors*. New York: Scholastic, 2012.

Glossary

bridge (brij) the ship's command center

cargo hold (KAHR-goh hohld) place to store goods carried by a ship

clergy (KLUR-jee) people who lead religious groups, like priests, ministers, and rabbis

crow's nest (KROHZ nest) a small platform used for a lookout, found on a ship's sailing mast

emigrants (EM-i-gruhntz) people who leave one country to settle in another

galley (GAL-ee) the kitchen on a boat

maritime (MAR-i-time) having to do with the sea

middle class (MID-uhl KLAS) people who are neither rich nor poor

ocean liners (OH-shuhn LYE-nurz) ships that run on a regular schedule from one seaport to another

steerage (STEER-ij) the part of a ship where passengers with the cheapest tickets slept, usually in the lower decks

stokers (STOH-kurz) people who tend the boilers on a steamship

transatlantic (tranz-ut-LAN-tik) crossing the Atlantic Ocean

Index

Page numbers in **bold** indicate illustrations.

About the Author

John H. Son is the author of *Finding My Hat*, a NYPL Best Book for the Teen Age about his adventures growing up in Texas as a boy of Korean descent. He is also the author of *If You Were a Kid on the Mayflower*, as well as the True Books *Relaxation and Yoga*, *Asia*, and *Elections: Why They Matter to You*. He lives with his wife and son in Brooklyn, New York.